For Your Wedding

T R A D I T I O N A L

G O W N S

For Your Wedding

TRADITIONAL

GOWNS

Amy M. Nebens

FRIEDMAN/FAIRFAX

A FRIEDMAN/FAIRFAX BOOK

© 2002 by Michael Friedman Publishing Group, Inc.

Please visit our website: www.metrobooks.com

Library of Congress Cataloging-in-Publication Data

Nebens, Amy.
    Traditional gowns / Amy Nebens.
       p. cm. -- (For your wedding)
    Includes bibliographical references and index.
    ISBN 1-58663-120-9 (alk. paper)
     1. Wedding costume.   I. Title.   II. Series.

TT663 .N43 2001
392.5′4--dc21

                                                            2001018993

Editor: Hallie Einhorn
Art Director: Jeff Batzli
Designer: Midori Nakamura
Photo Editor: Lori Epstein
Production Manager: Richela F. Morgan

Color separations by Fine Arts Repro House Co., Ltd.
Printed in China by C&C Offset Printing Co. Ltd.

1 3 5 7 9 10 8 6 4 2

Distributed by Sterling Publishing Company, Inc.
387 Park Avenue South
New York, NY 10016
Distributed in Canada by Sterling Publishing
Canadian Manda Group
One Atlantic Avenue, Suite 105
Toronto, Ontario, Canada M6K 3E7
Distributed in Australia by
Capricorn Link (Australia) Pty, Ltd.
P.O. Box 704, Windsor, NSW 2756 Australia

Front cover photograph: courtesy of Alfred Angelo

CONTENTS

INTRODUCTION

*A*s a bride takes her first step down the aisle, captivating her guests and her groom, the gown she wears—in that one glorious moment—sets the style and spirit of the event. When her dress is classic in form, borrowing its shape and details from eras past, she celebrates the timelessness inherent in wedding festivities and pays tribute to the unfailing endurance of romance.

What makes a gown traditional? It may be just one element or a combination of several that evokes the mood. Throughout the centuries, silhouettes, sleeve styles, necklines, fabrics, and trains have gone in and out of fashion, but a few have survived the trends of time and remain classics. The ball gown, for instance, typified by a small-waisted bodice and a billowing skirt, was made popular by Queen Victoria, who wore one at her marriage to Prince Albert in 1840. The style was also embraced by brides of the 1950s who favored Christian Dior's New Look. And today, proving to be forever fashionable, the ball gown is donned by brides who cherish its power to transform them into princesses for a day. But wearing a ball gown is not the only way for a bride to swathe herself in fairy-tale appeal. Sweetheart necklines, generous cathedral trains, and layers of delicate lace all promise to cast an enchanting air, just as they've done for generations of brides.

PAGE 6: CELEBRATING THE
ROMANCE OF THE DAY, A BALL
GOWN ENVELOPS A BRIDE IN
ELEGANCE AND STYLE. IN THIS
CYNTHIA C. & COMPANY
DESIGN, DAINTY CAP SLEEVES
AND A CORSETED BODICE ARE
SET OFF AGAINST THE SPLENDOR
OF A FULL BALL GOWN SKIRT
PUNCTUATED WITH INTRICATE
SILK FLOWERS.

OPPOSITE: THE FINE LINES
OF A SQUARE NECKLINE—
PERFECT FOR SHOWING OFF
A PROMINENT COLLARBONE—
ARE DELIGHTFULLY FRAYED BY
EDGES OF FRENCH LACE THAT
RISE FROM THE BODICE TO
PROVIDE ADDED EXCITEMENT
AROUND THE BRIDE'S FACE.
THE BODICE IS JOINED BY A
FULL TULLE SKIRT, WHICH
ENHANCES THE MAJESTIC
LOOK OF THE MANALÉ DRESS.

While many of today's designers create dresses in keeping with the pared-down fashions of the millennium, they also continue to offer time-honored styles. For even the most modern woman, with a closetful of the latest fashions, may see herself as a traditional bride and look to her gown to live out her bridal fantasies. She may dress every day for work in chic pantsuits, spend evenings out in trendy frocks, and while away the weekends in hip jeans and sleek ponytails. But when it comes to her wedding day, she wants to be the bride of her childhood visions. This desire can translate into a gown that is purely traditional in style or one that "marries" modern elements with classic features, perhaps a strapless bodice paired with a ballerina skirt. Whether she exchanges vows in the splendor of a grand ballroom or under the shade of a garden bower, the dress that a bride chooses will reveal her mood and her hopes and dreams for the day.

The powerful effect of the gown takes hold long before the wedding itself. As soon as you begin trying on dresses, swathed in yards and yards of silk and satin, you can't help but feel like a bride. Before you start shopping, though, you should make some planning decisions, which will in turn help you settle upon the right dress for you. If you are going to be married in winter, it's likely you won't want to wear a sleeveless number made of wispy organza; if the reception will be a casual event, perhaps held in your home, a flowing gown with layers of fabric might look out of place. That said, for this special occasion, go with your heart—any dress you fall in love with should be the one you choose no matter where or when you will be exchanging your vows.

OPPOSITE: MANY BUOYANT LAYERS ARE WORKING UNDER-COVER IN ORDER TO GIVE THIS CYNTHIA C. & COMPANY DRESS ITS STYLISH SHAPE. THE GENEROUS UNDERPINNINGS, FROM THE CRINOLINE TO THE PANTALOONS, NOT ONLY CREATE STRUCTURE FOR THE BALL GOWN, BUT ALSO LIFT THE HEM JUST SLIGHTLY OFF THE FLOOR TO REVEAL THE BRIDE'S BALLERINA-LIKE SHOES.

Start shopping for your gown as early as possible—a year in advance is not too soon. Often the salon or department store will have only sample sizes, and it can take as long as six months for a dress to be ordered or made and fitted. As you begin your search, keep an open mind; try on dresses with different types of silhouettes, sleeves, and necklines. Once you've seen yourself in a few, you—and a good salesperson—will begin to realize what styles you prefer and feel most comfortable wearing. It is also important to know what styles work best with your body type. An empire-waist dress or a ball gown with a Sabrina (or bateau) neckline works well for tall women with small chests; an A-line or princess shape with a V neck flatters petite, well-endowed brides. After you've chosen your gown, select shoes and undergarments; you'll want to have them on hand for your first fitting so that the seamstress can make the best possible alterations.

Some lucky brides wear gowns that are traditional in the truest sense—handed down by their mother, grandmother, or even future mother-in-law. If you have an heirloom dress that will be your "something old," it's important to follow the proper steps for restoring and altering the gown so that it fits well and looks its best. For starters, take the dress to a professional dry cleaner, one who specializes in wedding gown care and has experience handling the delicate fabric and embellishments. A professional should be able to get out most spots, even old white wine or champagne stains that were initially invisible but over time have oxidized into unsightly blemishes. The cleaner can also care for a dress with discolored fabric and restore it to its original pristine white.

When it comes to alterations, making an heirloom dress smaller is relatively simple. However, as each generation is a bit taller than the last, it's likely that an inherited wedding gown may be a few inches too short or too tight. While making a dress a size or two larger is a bit more involved, it certainly can be done. First check to see if your mother or grandmother saved any extra fabric from her alteration process that can be added back to the dress. If not, a good seamstress should be able to match the material closely, even doing some of her own handiwork where necessary. Be aware, though, that it will be difficult to match the color of the new fabric with the old, so the alterations will undoubtedly require some creativity and time, as well as added expense.

Whether you will be having a vintage dress cleaned just before the wedding or bringing home a new gown from a salon, once this prized garment is through your front door, you will want to ensure that it remains out of harm's way. Remove any plastic bag covering the gown; plastic is suitable only for short-term protection, as it can cause fabric to yellow if left on too long. Hang your dress, uncovered on a padded hanger, from a hook in the ceiling or at the top of a high door. You can also hide your dress in a closet, but in this case, cover it with a white cotton sheet, and leave plenty of room on either side so that it does not get wrinkled from being sandwiched in with other clothes.

After your wedding day, take the dress to a dry cleaner, again one who specializes in wedding attire; your dress will be cleaned, pressed, and stored—folded and wrapped in acid-free tissue and placed in an acid-free box to protect the fabric from yellowing. As an extra precaution against wrinkles, and for an

OPPOSITE: FOLDS OF TULLE, RIBBONS OF SATIN, ROWS OF PEARLS, EVEN PUFFS OF ROSE PETALS CREATE A ROMANTIC EXPLOSION OF WHITE AROUND A BRIDE ON HER WEDDING DAY. DEFINED PLEATS SAIL SMARTLY FROM THE STRAPLESS BODICE ALONG THE A-LINE SKIRT, CREATING A STREAMLINED EFFECT IN THE MIDST OF ALL THE FERVOR.

opportunity to sneak a look at your beloved garment, refold your dress once a year; when you do so, be sure to wear white cotton gloves so that the oils from your hands don't damage the material. Next to choosing the perfect dress, proper care is most important. After all, your treasured keepsake may one day become, for someone you love, a traditional gown.

RIGHT: IT'S THE SWEET DETAILS—LIKE THIS LEAFY DESIGN WINDING ITS WAY ACROSS THE BODICE OF A BRIDE'S GOWN—THAT MAKE A WEDDING DRESS SO SPECIAL. FOR A CHARMINGLY HARMONIOUS EFFECT, THE PETALS IN THE BRIDE'S BOUQUET ECHO THE DELICATE EMBROIDERED LEAVES.

OPPOSITE: A BRIDE'S GOWN BECOMES HER GOING-AWAY OUTFIT AS SHE AND HER GROOM RACE TO THEIR "GETAWAY CAR" IN THE STATION. DESPITE THE UNCONVENTIONAL EXIT, THE BRIDE'S DRESS HONORS TRADITION WITH ITS MODEST SLEEVES, ROMANTIC BALL GOWN SILHOUETTE, AND FROTHY UNDERSKIRT COMPLETE WITH LACE HEM.

CHAPTER ONE

FORMS THAT FLATTER

*W*hen you start the search for your wedding dress, the possibilities appear to be endless. But the quest becomes less daunting when you consider that many of today's gowns are inspired by one of five classic silhouettes—the A-line or princess, ballerina, ball gown, bustle back, or empire. The silhouette, or shape, is likely what you'll picture when imagining yourself in your wedding gown. And it is this vision that reveals your preference for the most fundamental element of your gown. The shape, after all, is what determines the personality of the dress—how it will look and the mood it will create—and, more importantly, how you'll feel when you're wearing it.

CLASSIC SILHOUETTES

A-line/Princess: Clean lines and a soft yet angular shape define the look of this style, which dates back to the 1920s and 1950s, when linear silhouettes were in vogue. Vertical seams that travel from the shoulders over a slightly tapered waist to the skirt create structure; a stiff fabric such as a heavy silk or brocade is best able to uphold the form. Because this cut is loose-fitting, it flatters most body types, from hourglass to full-figured, tall to petite. Many designers pair the classic A-line skirt with a strapless bodice or tank-style top for a somewhat updated take on traditional romance.

RIGHT: A SIMPLE LINE OF PIPING NEATLY DEFINES THE NATURAL WAIST IN THIS FIGURE-FLATTERING A-LINE GOWN BY AMSALE. WHILE THE BODICE SHINES IN SUPPLE DUCHESS SATIN, THE SKIRT IS MADE OF SILK GAZAR. THE OVERALL EFFECT IS SEAMLESS.

OPPOSITE: A FLOWING BEADED DESIGN ENCOURAGES THE EYE TO FOLLOW THE SMOOTH LINES OF THIS PRINCESS GOWN BY ALFRED ANGELO. THANKS TO A WHITE-ON-WHITE EFFECT, THE BEADING GLIDES OVER THE SOFT SATIN IN A QUIET RATHER THAN FLASHY MANNER. AN UPSWEPT HAIRSTYLE SHOWS OFF THE DRESS'S SCOOP NECK AND SHORT SLEEVES TO GREAT EFFECT, WHILE PRIM WHITE GLOVES ENHANCE THE LOOK OF INNOCENCE.

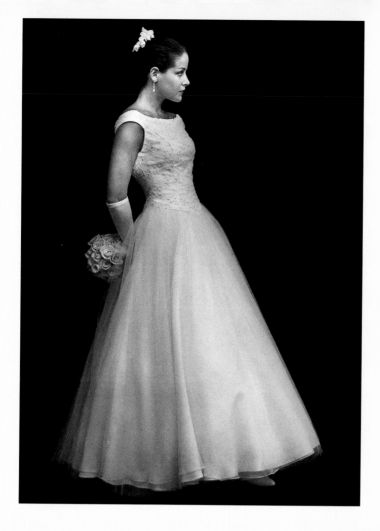

OPPOSITE: THIS PRINCESS GOWN BY ANNE BARGE LETS THE NATURAL SEAMS AND SILK MIKADO FABRIC DO ALL THE WORK. THE ONLY DETAILING NECESSARY IS THE HAND-EMBROIDERY OF METALLIC THREAD AND CRYSTAL BEADS AT THE SLEEVES AND HEM.

LEFT: TRADITIONAL FROM HEAD TO TOE, THIS WEDDING GOWN BY MANALÉ FEATURES A DELI-CATELY JEWELED BODICE OF SILK ORGANZA THAT SPILLS INTO A FLOWING BALLERINA SKIRT. JUST LIKE A DANCER, THE BRIDE WEARS HER HAIR UP, HELD IN PLACE BY A FEW SILK ROSES. ELBOW-LENGTH GLOVES ENHANCE THE TRADITIONAL TONE.

Ballerina: As its name suggests, this gown was inspired by the costumes worn by performers of classical ballet at the dawn of the twentieth century. A fitted bodice and dropped waist give way to a full skirt that stops just short of the ankles—allowing a pair of beautiful shoes to do more than just peek out from under the hem. Wispy fabrics such as tulle or lace cascade over crinoline or petti-coats, which give the dress its trademark flounce. All but the most petite bride will shine in the generous skirt, which along with the dropped waist, is a particularly popular means for camouflaging a woman's derrière or full hips.

RIGHT: BANDS OF LUMINOUS RIBBON, EACH FINISHED WITH A PRISTINE BOW IN BACK, ENCIRCLE A PUFF OF A BALL GOWN AS IF PREVENTING IT FROM TAKING FLIGHT. THE POWERFUL DETAILING IS ECHOED AT THE GOWN'S WAIST AND IN THE RUFFLED LAYERS OF THE VEIL.

OPPOSITE: THIS FLOWING ORGANZA BALL GOWN BY ALFRED ANGELO GAINS EVEN MORE BREADTH WITH THE ADDITION OF AN ORGANZA SHAWL, TRIMMED IN THE SAME EMBROIDERED SATIN AS THE SHIRRED SKIRT. THE SATIN BODICE, ACCENTED WITH BEADING, TAPERS INTO A TIGHT BASQUE WAISTLINE THAT FUR-THER DEFINES THE SKIRT'S SHAPE.

Ball gown: Visions of romance, tradition, and storybook weddings come to mind at the mere mention of the term *ball gown,* with its universally recognized billowing skirt springing from the dropped waist of a full bodice. The gown may have a horizontal seam at the waist or a basque waist, which features a V shape at the front. Summer brides often favor tulle-skirted ball gowns (winter brides may wear them too), but the most elaborate of these dresses are made from magical layers of supple silk taffeta. Like the ballerina gown, this style may overwhelm the petite bride, but it is perfect for the tall, slim bride who would like to highlight her curves. At the same time, the full skirt may benefit a bride who wants to mask her tummy or backside.

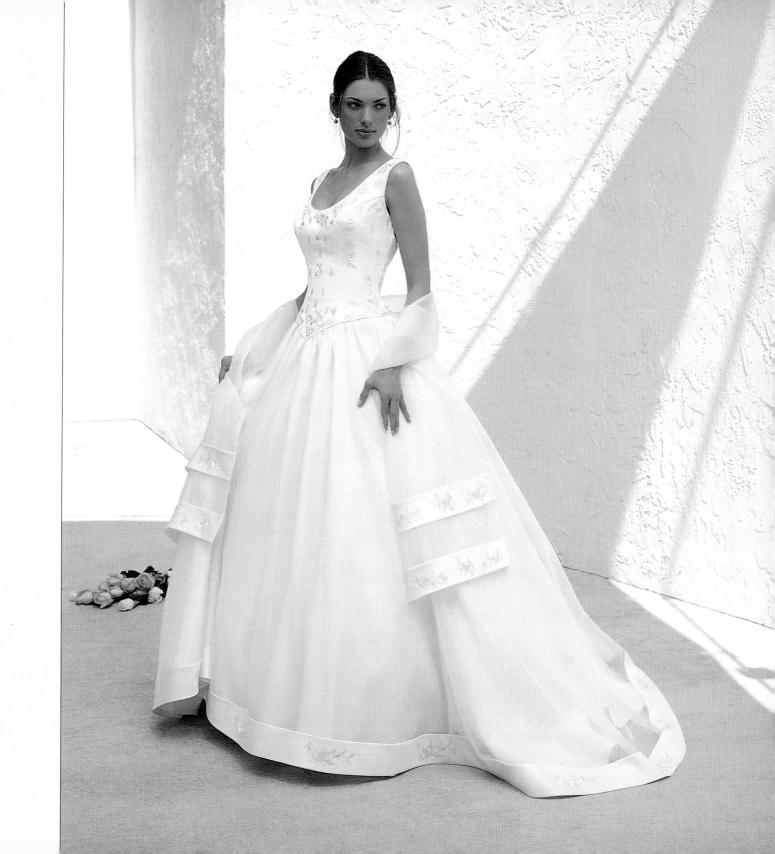

OPPOSITE: A BRIDE'S FIGURE
IS GENTLY FOLLOWED IN THE
STRAIGHT LINES OF THIS
EMPIRE-WAIST GOWN BY
ALFRED ANGELO. CRYSTAL
BEADING ON THE SLEEVES
AND SCOOP-NECK BODICE
ENHANCES THE AIRINESS
OF THE GEORGETTE SKIRT.
A DETACHABLE TRAIN LENDS
A TRADITIONAL LOOK WITHOUT
OVERDOING FORMALITY.

Bustle back: From the front, this type of gown can be deceiving—it may look to be just a simple column dress or a basic A-line gown. The drama lies in the back with yards of fabric whipped up into a frothy cloud, gathered up at the waist and trailing down the skirt. Whether the magnificent fabric sculpture is part of the original design or a beautiful and practical seamstress trick used to transform the gown from elegant altar wear to functioning party dress, its origins are clear: the bustle favored by fashionable ladies at the dawn of the twentieth century to lend curves to their forms. Today, this ornate embellishment is best for tall, slim brides who favor a bit more shape and won't get lost in all the fabric.

Empire: This gown is noted for its high, gathered waist and long, slim skirt. Although its name refers to the empire of Napoléon Bonaparte, whose wife Josephine wore this type of dress, the style can actually trace its origins back to ancient Greece and the column dresses fashionable during that era. Flowing fabrics such as organza and chiffon add to the allure of these airy, romantic gowns; popular, too, are delicate cap sleeves, typically set off against a scoop or square neckline. An empire-waist dress will detract from a high, thick waist; the gown's high waist will also enhance a small chest.

Remember, a dress that seems ideal in your dreams may not necessarily be the right one for you. Bring pictures from magazines or even old photographs to your bridal salon appointments in order to help describe what you are looking for, but be flexible. Try on your favorite styles first, then a few that you did not initially consider. A dress that did not do much for you on the hanger can become perfect the moment you slip it on.

IVORY SILK ORGANZA—
BEDECKED WITH AUSTRIAN
CRYSTALS AND BUGLE BEADS—
OVERLIES THE FITTED BODICE
OF THIS MELISSA SWEET A-LINE
GOWN, CREATING A SUBTLE
TONE-ON-TONE EFFECT. THE
BUSTLE BACK IMPARTS OLD-
FASHIONED CHARM, FONDLY
RECALLING AGES PAST.

THANKS TO A DAZZLING USE OF METALLIC EMBROIDERY ON THE BODICE OF THIS GIVENCHY EMPIRE-WAIST GOWN, THE PRINCESS-LINE ORGANZA SKIRT CAN BE LEFT UNADORNED. A TRIPLE POUF IN BACK ALLOWS THE BRIDE TO MAKE A GRAND ENTRANCE AND EXIT.

CHAPTER TWO

FITTING FRAMEWORK

Working hand in hand with the silhouette to create the allure of your gown, the neckline and sleeves dance beautiful patterns around your face, chest, neck, and arms. More than mere details, these components have a powerful effect on the overall impact of your dress, so give them careful consideration and attention.

As is the case with silhouettes, there are certain types of necklines and sleeves that exude romance and carry on tradition. The neckline can be plunging or high, scoop or square. It can enhance a décolletage, elongate a short neck, or flatter well-toned shoulders. Sleeves add drama and charm, depending on their length, their subtlety, their show. First determine the look that you want, then discover the details. Necklines and sleeves can be as simple as the most unadorned dress, lavishly embellished in keeping with an ornate gown, or lightly enhanced with delicate beading or embroidery along their hems and cuffs.

PAGE 30: THE SIMPLE SQUARE SCOOP NECK AND SHORT SLEEVES GIVE THIS ALFRED ANGELO DESIGN AN ALMOST CASUAL APPEARANCE—IF THAT'S POSSIBLE. BUT THE BEADED EMBROIDERY GIVES AWAY THE BRIDE'S DRESSY SECRET.

OPPOSITE: AN OTHERWISE SUBDUED GOWN BY CYNTHIA C. & COMPANY FINDS DRAMA IN ITS SHEER LONG SLEEVES. EACH FALLS LAZILY JUST BELOW THE SHOULDER AND EXTENDS DOWN TO THE WRIST, WHERE IT'S FINISHED OFF IN A FLARED, SATIN BELL CUFF ADORNED WITH A GRAND FLOWER.

LEFT: WITH ITS OPULENT COLLAR, FITTED SLEEVES, AND PILLBOX HEADPIECE, THIS ENSEMBLE RECALLS A TIME WHEN FASHION WAS ALL ABOUT FEMININITY. JUST AS RELEVANT TO TODAY'S BRIDE, THOUGH, THE WIDE PORTRAIT COLLAR PROVIDES THE OPPORTUNITY TO SHOW OFF WELL-DEFINED SHOULDERS. THE DETAILING ON THE COLLAR IS REPEATED ALONG THE HEMLINE OF THIS CYNTHIA C. & COMPANY GOWN FOR A POLISHED LOOK.

TRADITIONAL NECKLINES

High: This style can vary from a rounded hem at the base of the neck to a band that sits higher, fitting like a mock turtleneck. Often the lower version will be found on a sleeveless or halter gown—a mix of classic and contemporary design; the highest necklines, which are the most dramatic, are typically paired with straight long sleeves. A well-endowed bride who wants a bit of coverage might, at first, consider this style, though she will find that the long bodice (straight up to the neck) actually accentuates her chest. Thanks to this effect, a small-chested bride can fare quite well with a high neckline. A tall, slender bride who is going for a bit of glamour might also turn to this style, while a woman with broad shoulders might opt for the halter look in particular.

Off-the-shoulder: This type of neckline, which rests just below the shoulders and flows into the sleeves of a gown, is at once stunning and feminine, as it allows more than just a glimpse of a bride's shoulders and collarbone. The revealing style, ultimately most flattering to a bride with a full bustline, can cut straight across the chest or take on a sweetheart shape (see page 39).

Portrait: For those brides who desire an off-the-shoulder look but seek slightly more coverage, this style—a scoop neck that grazes the tips of both shoulders—will fit the bill. Like the off-the-shoulder, the portrait collar shows off a bride's well-toned upper body, but it has a bit more fabric around the neckline. It was the choice of Queen Victoria, as well as of the many brides who zealously emulated her style during the early Victorian era.

RIGHT: LACY THREE-QUARTER
SLEEVES AND A FLIRTY SABRINA
NECKLINE COVER A BRIDE IN
ULTRAFEMININE SPLENDOR.
IN CONTRAST, THE CIRCLE
SKIRT OF THIS ALFRED ANGELO
DESIGN IS UNADORNED (AND
QUITE MODEST), AS IS THE
DETACHABLE TRAIN.

OPPOSITE: THIS SLEEVELESS
REEM ACRA GOWN IS PERFECT
FOR CALLING ATTENTION TO A
BRIDE'S SHAPELY SHOULDERS
AND SLENDER NECK. AN
EMBROIDERED MOSAIC PATTERN
PROVIDES BEAUTIFUL DETAILING
FROM THE BATEAU NECKLINE TO
THE DROPPED WAIST, WHERE
INVERTED PLEATS TAKE OVER
TO CREATE A SCULPTED AND
FULL SKIRT.

Sabrina: The shape of this neckline is the same in front as it is in back; the lines of the Sabrina (or bateau) echo the contours of the collarbone, from just below the top of one shoulder straight across the chest to the other, for a look that is subtly sexy yet sophisticated. The straight, wide hem reveals little if any cleavage—a quality that is most beneficial to small-chested brides.

OPPOSITE: ON A DAY THAT'S ALL ABOUT ROMANCE, WHY NOT A NECKLINE NAMED FOR THE OCCASION? MANALÉ'S PLUNGING SWEETHEART NECK-LINE IS UPDATED WITH LONG ILLUSION SLEEVES DETAILED IN LATTICEWORK. THE A-LINE SKIRT IS MORE STRUCTURED THAN A FLOWING BALL GOWN BUT STILL LOOSE ENOUGH TO SUIT MOST FIGURE TYPES.

LEFT: BEADED ALENÇON LACE DRAWS THE EYE TO THE SCOOP NECK OF THIS CHARMING GOWN BY PRISCILLA OF BOSTON. THE CAPTIVATING EMBELLISHMENT REAPPEARS AT THE DROPPED WAIST, THEREBY FRAMING THE BODICE.

Scoop: This popular U-shaped neckline—often a mirror image in front and back—is a favorite of many brides and designers who appreciate its classic look. The scoop can also be square or cut in the shape of a V, the latter revealing a bit more décolletage.

Sweetheart: This neckline is certainly sweet—and shaped just like the top of a heart. The gently curved lines may be designed in an on- or off-the-shoulder style, and as the neckline has a tendency to be revealing, it is best suited to well-endowed brides. For those who want to show a bit less, designers can "build up" the neckline with fabric or embellishment to provide more coverage. The addition of a sheer material, referred to as illusion, is another possibility for brides who want to feel less exposed yet maintain the stylish effect.

RIGHT: ELEGANT IN ITS SIM-
PLICITY, THIS MANALÉ GOWN
FEATURES A FITTED BODICE
WITH TWO PRINCESS SEAMS
THAT FLOW SMOOTHLY DOWN
TO THE DROPPED WAIST AND
SOFT A-LINE SKIRT. PEARLS
STRUNG ALONG THE SCOOP
NECKLINE OFFER A TOUCH OF
UNDERSTATED GLAMOUR.

OPPOSITE: THE CAP SLEEVES
AND SOMEWHAT ROUNDED
SQUARE NECKLINE OF THIS
MELISSA SWEET DESIGN ARE
WINSOME DETAILS FOR A
DEMURE BRIDE. THE DROP-
WAIST BODICE—ENCRUSTED
WITH EMBROIDERY, BUGLE
BEADS, RHINESTONES, AND
CRYSTALS—SENDS OFF A
SOPHISTICATED SPARK.

TIME-HONORED SLEEVES

Cap: A dressed-up T-shirt sleeve, this style is more fitted, more rounded, and more revealing than its casual cousin and is perfect for a bride who wants just a hint of coverage. Because it conceals only minimally, this sleeve is best for brides with well-toned shoulders and upper arms. On most dresses, the cap sleeve can be worn on or off the shoulder, depending on what is most comfortable.

OPPOSITE: THE BRIDE'S TIARA MIRRORS THE DESIGN SEEN IN THE NECKLINE, SLEEVES, AND HEM OF HER CHRISTOS GOWN. DELICATE BEADING AND SOUTACHE TRIM ENHANCE A REVEALING SCOOP NECK AND PLAYFUL CAP SLEEVES. SIDE PLEATS ALONG THE GENEROUS SATIN BALL GOWN GIVE IT MORE VOLUME, WHILE BEADING AT THE HEM CREATES ADDITIONAL DRAMA.

LEFT: THIS BRIDE IS NOT AN ILLUSION, ALTHOUGH HER DRESS PUTS THAT DESIGN TOOL TO WONDERFUL USE. HER SHEER SHORT SLEEVES AND JEWEL NECKLINE ARE RIMMED IN TINY SOUTACHE DETAILING; THE WAISTLINE, HEM, AND APRON FRONT BORROW THE SAME DAINTY ACCENT. RATHER THAN DETRACTING FROM THE CHRISTOS DRESS, THE FLOWER APPLIQUÉS ON THE SHEER, LONG VEIL HELP TO LEND A TOUCH OF MYSTERY.

SHORT SLEEVES ARE NOT NEC-
ESSARILY CASUAL, ESPECIALLY
WHEN MADE OF DECADENT
DUCHESS SATIN AND PAIRED
WITH OPERA-LENGTH GLOVES.
CYNTHIA C. & COMPANY
FURTHER DRESSES UP THIS
BALL GOWN WITH AN EXQUISITE
COMBINATION OF BEADING AND
EMBROIDERY THAT CREATES A
CINCHED EFFECT AT THE WAIST
AND THEN GENTLY TRICKLES
DOWN TO HIGHLIGHT THE
SKIRT'S DRAPE. A CLEAN ROW
OF OPALESCENT BUTTONS
DANCES UP THE BACK.

ALL DRESSED UP WITH THE
MOST IMPORTANT PLACE TO
GO. AN OFF-THE-SHOULDER
SLEEVE DANGLING FROM A
FITTED BODICE MAKES A
DELIGHTFUL COMPLEMENT FOR
A FLOWING BALL GOWN SKIRT.
PROMINENT SEAMS, A STRING
OF PEARLS, AND LONG GLOVES
ENHANCE THE STYLE. TO COM-
PLETE THE LOOK, A TIERED VEIL
FOLLOWS THE FULL LINES OF
THE GOWN'S SILHOUETTE.

OPPOSITE: FORMFITTING LONG
SLEEVES EXTEND THE CANVAS
FOR AN ELABORATE BEADED
DESIGN THAT MAKES ITS WAY
ACROSS THE BODICE. WHILE THE
OVERALL STYLE OF THE DRESS
PROJECTS A SOMEWHAT QUIET
AND RESERVED LOOK—REFLECT-
ING THE SOLEMNITY OF THE
OCCASION—THE GLITTERING
DETAILS INJECT A FESTIVE NOTE.

Long sleeves: Whether a bride completely covers her arms for the result-ing look, for warmth, or for religious considerations, there are many beautiful styles from which to choose. Simple or embellished, close-fitting or loose and flowing, this type of sleeve will likely hide any perceived flaws and flatter arms of all shapes and sizes. Following are three variations on the style.

Juliet: When you picture the most traditional, opulent ball gown, it's likely that the sleeves take on this shape: long and formfitting with a dramatic puff at the shoulders. The charming puffs can be quite elaborate or more demure, but either way, the look tends to overwhelm petite brides, who drown in all the fabric.

Leg-of-mutton: During the second half of the nineteenth century, when fashion was all about practicality and simplicity, the leg-of-mutton (or gigot) sleeve enjoyed its heyday. Today, it brings a sentimental touch of yesteryear to a gown. A full sleeve (gathered or loose) flows from the shoulder to the elbow; from just below the elbow to the wrist, the fabric is tapered to the arm.

Bell: Expressing pure romance, as befits the wedding day, this sleeve fits close to the arm from the shoulder to just above the elbow, where the fabric then fans out into a soft flare that cascades to just above the wrist. Thanks to this design, the lower part of the sleeve has a fluid quality, swaying smoothly with each step the bride takes. This enchanting style is beautiful with an off-the-shoulder gown and works best in a light, airy fabric such as organza or a fine lace.

RIGHT: THIS REFINED BALL GOWN BY MANALÉ EMBRACES SO MANY ELEMENTS OF CLASSIC STYLE THAT IT IS SURE TO APPEAL TO MANY A BRIDE. THE DRAMATIC SCOOP NECK GIVES WAY TO A FITTED DROP-WAIST BODICE WITH LONG, ELEGANT SLEEVES, EACH FASTENED WITH A SLEEK ROW OF BUTTONS. THE OTHERWISE UNADORNED BODICE IS EDGED WITH SATIN CORD, WHILE BOX PLEATS ENLIVEN THE SKIRT.

OPPOSITE: THE BELL SLEEVES OF THIS CYNTHIA C. & COMPANY DRESS OFFER A HINT OF DRAMA AS THEY FLARE OUT AT THE WRISTS, GENTLY ALLUDING TO THE SHAPE OF THE BALL GOWN SKIRT. BOTH THE SOFT FLUIDITY OF THE FABRIC AND THE DELI-CATE FLORAL EMBROIDERY SERVE TO PLAY UP THE BRIDE'S FEMININITY. THE EFFECT OF THE LACY BODICE AND SLEEVES BECOMES ALL THE MORE POW-ERFUL WHEN THEY'RE PAIRED WITH AN UNEMBELLISHED SKIRT OF DUCHESS SATIN.

Three-quarter: Conjuring up all the splendor of 1950s glamour, this style, which extends from the shoulder to the midway point between the elbow and wrist, is an alluring alternative to long sleeves. Brides can be a bit exposed while leaving something to the imagination.

Necklines and sleeve styles can be mixed and matched—with each other and with different gown silhouettes. Again, allow yourself to explore the possibilities until you find the one that best suits you.

RIGHT: IN THIS TWO-PIECE ENSEMBLE BY CAROLINA HERRERA, THREE-QUARTER SLEEVES ARE EMBROIDERED AT THE HEMS AND FRINGED WITH DROP-PEARL BEADING; THE SAME DETAILING DISGUISES THE POINT WHERE THE TOP MEETS THE SKIRT.

OPPOSITE: IN THIS L'EZU GOWN, THE REVEALING NATURE OF THE SQUARE NECKLINE IS CONTINUED IN THE V-SHAPED OPENING AT THE END OF EACH THREE-QUARTER SLEEVE. THE CORSETED BODICE HAS A SLIMMING EFFECT, WHILE TEAMS OF PLEATS AND SEAMS ADD FULLNESS TO AN ALREADY BILLOWY SKIRT.

IN THIS ENSEMBLE BY GIVENCHY, A DELICATE SILK ORGANZA WRAP, TRIMMED IN LUSTROUS SILK SATIN, BRINGS MODESTY TO A HALTER GOWN BY COVERING THE BRIDE'S BARE ARMS AND SHOULDERS. THANKS TO THE TWO-PIECE DESIGN, A BRIDE DESIRING A SLEEVELESS DRESS CAN DANCE IN THE GOWN OF HER DREAMS YET STILL FEEL APPROPRIATELY ATTIRED FOR A FORMAL OR RELIGIOUS CERE-MONY. METALLIC EMBROIDERY CREATES EYE-CATCHING DETAILS AROUND THE NECKLINE OF THE DRESS, WHILE BOX PLEATS SEWN INTO THE SKIRT GIVE THE BALL GOWN ITS SHAPELY FLARE.

A DUCHESS SATIN OVERCOAT
WITH THREE-QUARTER SLEEVES
AND A REGAL MINK COLLAR
PROVIDES ELEGANT COVERAGE
FOR A BRIDE WEARING A
TANK-STYLE SHEATH UNDER-
NEATH. THE LATTER WILL BE
UNVEILED AT THE RECEPTION.
BOTH PIECES ARE DESIGNED
BY CAROLINA HERRERA.

CHAPTER THREE

TEXTURES
AND TRIMMINGS

The fabric of your gown, the various embellishments, and the dressmaker's techniques all go a long way toward making you feel, and sometimes sound, like a bride. Take the soft rustle of a taffeta ball gown that whispers in tune with the wedding march as you make your way down the aisle, the subtle sparkle of crystal beads that add shine to your already radiant glow, or the cheerful flounce of a pleated skirt that mirrors your blissful smile. The fabric of a gown also works together with the silhouette, helping to establish its structure whether it be a classic starched form or a flowing design.

Soft and silky, light and breezy, or crisp and formal—for centuries there have been so many wonderful choices. Which is the right one for you? Your decision may well depend on the season of your wedding or the cost, but most likely it will come down to your answer to one simple question: Do you envision yourself wrapped in folds of lavish, heavy fabric or draped in layers of sheer, ethereal gossamer?

PAGE 54: EMBROIDERED SWIRLS PUNCTUATED WITH PEARLS AND BEADS SEEM TO DANCE IN THE SUNLIGHT WHILE BRINGING EXQUISITE TEXTURE TO A BALL GOWN. THE TANK-STYLE BODICE LENDS A MODERN FEEL TO THE FULL, PLEATED SKIRT.

OPPOSITE: FRILLY ROWS OF FRENCH LACE SPECKLED WITH BUGLE BEADS, PEARLS, AND CRYSTAL ADORN THE BODICE OF THIS MANALÉ DRESS. THE EMBELLISHMENTS COME TO A HALT AT THE WAISTLINE, WHERE A GAZAR A-LINE SKIRT TAKES OVER. THANKS TO THIS ABSENCE OF ORNAMENTATION, THE INHERENT BEAUTY OF THE SILK FABRIC CAN SHINE.

LEFT: ORGANZA AND SATIN FORM A BLISSFUL UNION IN THIS ALFRED ANGELO DESIGN. MATTE SATIN ORGANZA IS USED FOR THE SLEEVELESS V-NECKED BODICE, WHICH ENDS AT A BASQUE WAISTLINE. WIDE SATIN BANDS ENCIRCLE THE SHIRRED ORGANZA SKIRT, WHICH, THOUGH FULL, IS LIGHTWEIGHT AND NOT AT ALL ENCUMBERING.

CLASSIC FABRICS

Brocade: The epitome of texture, this fabric is typified by its raised designs. For a luxurious effect, brocade can be used for the entire dress; it can also be employed to create rich accents at the neck, skirt hem, or sleeves. The texture of the fabric, which is woven on Jacquard looms, is created at the moment the fabric is made; it's not an embellishment added later. Depending on the setting of the loom, the pattern may be linear or curvy, elaborate or sedate.

RIGHT: THIS TOMASINA GOWN PROVIDED INSPIRATION FOR THE BRIDE'S BOUQUET. PINK ROSETTES ACCENT A SWEETHEART NECKLINE AND CURLICUES OF PIPING THAT GLIDE OVER THE SILK SATIN SKIRT. THE SILK FLOWERS ADD A DASH OF COLOR, AS WELL AS DIMENSION.

OPPOSITE: DELICATE BOWS—EACH TIPPED WITH AN AUSTRIAN CRYSTAL IN THE CENTER—ARE WOVEN ALL OVER THE SILK JACQUARD OF THIS TOMASINA BALL GOWN TO CREATE A LOOK THAT IS AS DELIGHTFUL AS THE PRETTIEST WRAPPED PRESENT. A GENEROUS BOW IN BACK HAS LONG TAILS THAT TRAIL PAST THE HEM OF THE REGAL GOWN.

Lace: The most magical and delicate of fabrics, lace may be crafted by hand or by machine in patterns that are innumerable and undeniably romantic. In the true sense of tradition, most laces are named for the European city in which they were originally made. The amazing variety includes Alençon, Chantilly, Duchesse, and Lyons, to name a few. Styles range from intricate to simple, heavy to airy, floral to swirling; the stitching can stand on its own or be re-embroidered with a light outline. While one bride may favor a gown completely covered in lace, another may choose to incorporate this traditional fabric in just one detail of her dress or in an accessory, such as a veil or a pair of gloves. Some women even include antique lace in their gowns, thereby paying homage to weddings past.

Silk: Almost all brides wear a dress of silk—in one form or another. From crisp faille to misty chiffon, the numerous types vary according to weight and texture, depending on the weaving technique used. Rich fabrics such as duchess satin and taffeta are extravagant in appearance and lush in texture. Because they add markedly to the architecture of a gown, these types of silk are typically used to form the sensational flare of a princess dress, the majestic posture of a ball gown, or the surprise decoration of a bustle. Wispy charmeuse satin, chiffon, and organza create delicate silhouettes with sheer beauty and gentle illusions. Thanks to the advent of nylon in the 1950s, many of these looks and textures can be simulated to provide a less expensive (and sometimes hardier) alternative to silk.

OPPOSITE: THE BODICE OF THIS GOWN BY ALFRED ANGELO IS ENCASED IN RE-EMBROIDERED LACE AND BEADING FOR A LOOK THAT IS SIMPLY BREATHTAKING. TO CREATE A SENSE OF CONTINUITY, THE SAME RIVETING COMBINATION OF DETAILS SPILLS DOWN THE BACK OF THE SATIN A-LINE SKIRT, ALONG THE CENTER PANEL. A STRING OF DELICATE BUTTONS FINISHES THE EFFECT.

LEFT: IF A BRIDE SHOULD SHINE ON HER WEDDING DAY, SO SHOULD HER DRESS. THIS CYNTHIA C. & COMPANY GOWN ALLOWS A BRIDE TO REVEL IN THE LUMINESCENCE OF SILK SATIN. WHILE THE SHEEN OF THE FABRIC IS SOFTENED SLIGHTLY BY BEADWORK ON THE BODICE, IT COMES THROUGH FULL FORCE IN THE LAVISH PLEATED SKIRT.

THE MANY LOOKS OF SILK
SATIN ORGANZA REFLECT THE
FLURRY OF A BRIDE'S FEELINGS.
IN THIS MANALÉ DESIGN,
SKINNY PLEATS FLOWING FROM
THE RAGLAN SLEEVES TO THE
SQUARE NECK AND DOWN THE
FITTED BODICE GIVE WAY TO
PINCHED PLEATS AND A SOFT,
FLUID SKIRT. A FEW SMALL
BLOSSOMS DANGLE FROM A SILK
FLOWER FASTENED IN BACK; A
SIMILAR FLOWER ADORNS THE
BRIDE'S HAIR.

FOR CENTURIES, BRIDES HAVE WORN PEARLS ON THEIR WEDDING DAY. THIS SILK SATIN MANALÉ GOWN TAKES THE TRADITION TO A WHOLE NEW LEVEL WITH A SCOOP NECK ENCRUSTED IN PEARLS AND A MATCHING BAND AT THE WAISTLINE. THANKS TO THE BEADING, NO NECKLACE IS NECESSARY.

Tulle: Like the prettiest tutu of a ballerina or a gown for a royal princess, a bride's wedding dress seems naturally to call for this fanciful material. Open-weave tulle can be made from silk, cotton, nylon, or rayon and treated many different ways to create a soft or stiff finish or something in between. The results vary to form everything from a starched ball gown to a froth of petticoats to the airiest veil or overlay.

OPPOSITE: FORMED FROM 150 YARDS (137M) OF FABRIC, THE SKIRT OF THIS MANALÉ GOWN—A VERITABLE CLOUD OF TULLE—IS SURE TO TURN ANY WEDDING DAY INTO A BRIDAL FANTASY. BY PAIRING THE FROTHY SKIRT WITH A SATIN CORDED BODICE COVERED IN RHINESTONES THAT TWINKLE LIKE STARS, THE DRESS ACHIEVES A TRULY MAGICAL EFFECT.

LEFT: THE PERFECT EMBELLISHMENT TO ANY GOWN IS ONE THAT COMPLEMENTS WITHOUT OVERWHELMING. THE LUSTROUS PEARLS THAT TRAIL ALONG THE SCOOP NECKLINE AND SLEEVES OF THIS BALL GOWN ARE SET OFF AGAINST THE FABRIC'S SHEEN. A DAINTY BOW ADDS A SUBTLE FLAIR, AS DOES THE RIBBON TRIM OF THE BRIDE'S VEIL.

OPPOSITE: AN ASYMMETRICAL
PANEL GIVES THIS L'EZU DRESS
A SENSE OF PANACHE. HIGH-
LIGHTED BY A SLIM STREAM OF
DELICATELY BEADED EMBROIDERY,
THIS UNIQUE ELEMENT IS
CERTAIN TO GARNER ATTENTION.

Velvet: The soft, plush pile of velvet envelops a bride in pure luxury. It is best reserved for the grandest gowns that can make the most of the fabric's weight. Because the fabric is so heavy, it is favored almost exclusively for cold-weather weddings. Imagine a stunning white velvet bodice, draped skirt, or warm wrap contributing to the effect of an enchanting winter wonderland.

Choose your fabric for the season, your senses, your desires, and then look to the design techniques and the decorations—with these in place, the dress takes on its final form. A bevy of ruffles jazzes up a hemline; two simple seams create a slimming waistline; a pleat in back conceals a flounce that becomes visible as a bride takes each step down the aisle. Appliqués, perhaps taking the form of spring-like flowers fashioned from silk or lace, can completely cover the bodice or trail gingerly along the hem. The same holds true for other embellishments such as Austrian crystals, iridescent glass beads, and tiny white pearls. Fine silk thread can create embroidered designs on the fabric and add a whisper of color to the dress, while cording may be used around the stitchwork to achieve a raised outline. For a whimsical touch, fringe will inject a festive note at the end of a cuff or hem. All of these trimmings, many hand-sewn by talented artisans, have been relished by brides since wedding attire became fashionable and look equally beautiful and timeless today.

FABRIC CAN CREATE WONDROUS GOWNS AND STRIKING ADORNMENTS. HERE, A GENEROUS FABRIC BOW BECOMES A STUNNING AND FITTING ADDITION TO AN ORNATE DRESS BEARING INTRICATE PATTERNS OF EMBROIDERY AND BEADING.

FASHION TURNS TO FUNCTION
IN THIS CHIC GOWN, WHICH
FEATURES TANTALIZING LACING
AS A SEXY ALTERNATIVE TO
BUTTONS OR A ZIPPER. AT THE
WAISTLINE, A FLOWER BURSTS
INTO FULL BLOOM, SUGGESTING
THE PROMISE OF THE DAY
WHILE HOLDING A SHINY FOLD
IN PLACE.

RIGHT: OFTEN THE TINIEST DETAILS MAKE THE BIGGEST IMPACT. THIS ALFRED ANGELO A-LINE GOWN REPEATS A SIMPLE PATTERN—A TRIPLE ROW OF BOWS—AT THE SLEEVES, ON THE BODICE, AND AT THE HEM. IN KEEPING WITH THE CLEAN LINES OF THE DRESS, THE EMBELLISH-MENTS CREATE A LOOK THAT IS GIRLY BUT NOT AT ALL FUSSY.

OPPOSITE: HAND-PAINTED FLOWERS BRING HINTS OF COLOR TO AN OTHERWISE TRADITIONAL WHITE GOWN BY ALFRED ANGELO. THANKS TO THE DELICATE PASTEL HUES, THE DRESS HAS THE REFRESHING QUALITY OF A SPRING DAY.

CHAPTER FOUR

ELEGANT ENDINGS

You're standing in front of the mirror at the salon, thinking you might have found your dress: the silhouette is perfect, the neckline and sleeves oh-so becoming, and the fabric and embellishments divine. But wait. Before you make any final decisions, what about the train? Far from an afterthought, the train is an integral part of a dress's design and, hence, an important factor in your bridal style. After all, as you glide past your guests at the start of the ceremony they will get only a fleeting look at you from the front, then watch your back as you proceed to the altar, meet your groom, and exchange your wedding vows. Do you want to make a powerful statement with a trailing monarch gown, popular at royal weddings for generations? Or would you prefer the understated grace of a sweep train that just barely grazes the floor?

The train may be part of the gown or a separate length of detachable fabric. If the former, the train can be bustled after the ceremony, allowing you to move about the reception relatively unencumbered. To lay the groundwork for a bustle, a seamstress will sew hidden buttons, loops, hooks, or snaps at the back of the waist and corresponding elements at the hem of the skirt. Depending on the method used to fold and roll the fabric, the bustle can have sensational or subdued flourishes, from swags to bows to flowers. If the train is exceptionally short, it can even be bustled under the gown and hidden away. Some brides forgo the bustle, preferring to "carry" the train by a fabric loop that is sewn on the underside of the gown and then slipped over the wrist during the reception. You would only want to do this for

RIGHT: RICH DUCHESS SILK GETS AN AIRY INFLECTION FROM THE TULLE INSERT OF A FRENCH BUTTERFLY TRAIN. THE BUSTLE SEEMS TO BE HELD IN PLACE AT THE WAIST BY A CHARMING BOW—A WHIMSICAL DETAIL AGAINST THE HAND-BEADED AND EMBROIDERED BODICE OF THIS CLEA COLET GOWN.

OPPOSITE: A DETACHABLE HAND-EMBROIDERED TRAIN, BANDED WITH SILK SATIN, MAKES A BRIDE AS BEAUTIFUL TO LOOK AT FROM THE BACK AS FROM THE FRONT. WHEN THE TRAIN IS REMOVED FOR THE RECEPTION, REMINDERS OF ITS BRILLIANCE LINGER, AS THE DELICATE EMBROIDERY OF BUTTERCUP FLOWERS— ACCENTED WITH BUGLE BEADS AND SEED BEADS—IS REPEATED IN THE EMPIRE BODICE OF THIS JANELL BERTÉ GOWN.

the shortest of trains made from a lightweight fabric—otherwise you will feel as though you're carrying a burden. Remember, comfort is of the utmost importance, as you want to be able to enjoy your special day. Detachable trains—held in place with snaps, buttons, hooks, or Velcro—are favored by brides who want a traditional profile for the walk down the aisle but desire a more minimal look for the party afterward.

Brides of earlier times would choose their train style to correspond with the significance of the celebration and their position in society. You will want to choose a train that befits the style of your dress and your size: lengthy trains, for instance, look best with the most formal gowns. A petite bride is better off with a shorter train that keeps everything in proportion.

RIGHT: A TWO-PIECE ENSEMBLE
AFFORDS A BRIDE VERSATILITY
ON HER WEDDING DAY. THIS
JESSICA MCCLINTOCK DESIGN
PAIRS A SHEER SHRUG OF
EMBROIDERED NETTING WITH
A STRAPLESS BUSTIER GOWN.
THE EMPIRE WAIST, LONG SKIRT,
AND SWEEP TRAIN BEAR THE
SAME EMBROIDERED DESIGN
FOR A SEAMLESS EFFECT.

OPPOSITE: GLORIOUS VENISE
LACE DRESSES UP THE BODICE
OF THIS GALINA GOWN AND
THEN MAKES AN ENCORE
APPEARANCE AT THE BASE OF
THE CHAPEL TRAIN. THE TONE-
ON-TONE DETAILING MAINTAINS
THE AIRY FEELING OF THE WISPY
ORGANZA FABRIC.

TRADITIONAL TRAINS

Sweep: The shortest train, this style flows from the waist and just barely touches the floor.

Court: Popular with Victorian brides who began patterning their gowns after royal attire, this train extends about three feet (90cm) from the waist of the gown.

Chapel: This style, which runs about four feet (1.2m) from the waist, is long enough to create drama, but not too long for a less formal gown or a petite bride.

RIGHT: THE CHAPEL TRAIN OF THIS JANELL BERTÉ DRESS SEEMS TO QUIETLY CAST ITSELF AWAY FROM THE FITTED BODICE. WHILE THE BODICE IS EDGED IN PINK AND ROSE-COLORED DAISIES ACCENTED WITH SWAROVSKI CRYSTALS, THE TRAIN IS FINISHED WITH BUTTONS.

OPPOSITE: THE SLEEK SHEEN OF DUCHESS SATIN FLOWS FROM THE TOP OF THIS SLEEVELESS CLEA COLET BALL GOWN TO THE GRACEFUL SWAY OF ITS CHAPEL TRAIN. THE SWEEPING LINES OF THE FANNED-OUT TRAIN SEEM TO MIRROR THOSE OF THE PLUNGING BACK, WHICH IS FASTENED BY A ROW OF BUTTONS ENDING IN A CLUSTER OF FRENCH COUTURE FLOWERS.

Cathedral: More appropriate for formal celebrations, this train can run six to eight feet (1.8–2.4m) long, starting from the waist of the gown.

Monarch: Also referred to as an "extended" or "royal cathedral" train, the monarch train has long been the choice of royalty, beginning with Queen Victoria in 1840. Typically, the length of this train is about twelve feet (3.7m), though ones as long as eighteen (5.5m) or even twenty feet (6.1m) are not unheard of.

Watteau: A wispy train, this style attaches to the shoulders of a gown and floats down to the floor.

OPPOSITE: THE MANY LAYERS OF THIS GOWN, AS SUMPTUOUS AS THE TIERS ON A WEDDING CAKE, FLOW NATURALLY INTO EACH OTHER, CREATING A TRAIN THAT STRETCHES FAR BEYOND THE BOUNDARIES OF THE HEM. A CATHEDRAL-LENGTH TULLE VEIL CASCADES OVER THE OPULENT CONFECTION LIKE THE THINNEST LAYER OF ICING.

LEFT: AN AIRY COMBINATION OF TULLE AND LACE SPRINGS FROM THE BACK OF THIS PAT KERR DESIGN, CREATING A WATTEAU TRAIN THAT SEEMS AT HOME IN THE BREEZE. A MATCHING HEADPIECE ADDS TO THE DREAMY EFFECT.

RIGHT: A CHIC A-LINE GOWN
BY CYNTHIA C. & COMPANY
BECOMES ALL THE MORE STYLISH
WITH THE HELP OF TWO TAILS
THAT SAIL OVER A GRACEFUL
CHAPEL TRAIN. AT THE END OF
EACH TAIL, AN INTRICATE BLEND
OF EMBROIDERY AND BEADING
CREATES AN ELEGANT FINALE.
THE EXQUISITE DETAILING
MIRRORS THAT OF THE BODICE
AND SLEEVES.

OPPOSITE: A CYNTHIA C. &
COMPANY COLUMN DRESS THAT
RECALLS THE PAST RECEIVES
ADDED APPEAL WITH A DETACH-
ABLE TRAIN THAT FLOWS FROM
A RUCHED WAIST. OFFERING
THE BEST OF BOTH WORLDS,
THE LIGHTWEIGHT TRAIN—
MADE OF STRETCH JERSEY—
CAN BE WORN DURING THE
CEREMONY FOR A FORMAL
TOUCH, THEN REMOVED TO
GIVE THE BRIDE A MORE
RELAXED, THOUGH STILL
REFINED, AIR.

OPPOSITE: ENROBED IN SHEER
SPLENDOR, A BRIDE IS QUEEN
FOR A DAY WEARING AN
ALFRED ANGELO SATIN GOWN
COVERED IN HAND-BEADED
RE-EMBROIDERED LACE THAT
MAKES ITS WAY FROM A
SCALLOPED BODICE AND
SLEEVES DOWN TO THE END
OF A LUXURIOUS TRAIN. THE
DETAILING CREATES A LACY
STREAM IN BACK, WHILE
A LONG ROW OF BUTTONS
SKIPS DOWN THE CENTER AS
THOUGH PARTING THE WATERS.

LEFT: A ROW OF SOFT ROSETTES
DOES MORE THAN EMBELLISH
THIS GOWN; IT CAMOUFLAGES
THE POINT WHERE THE TRAIN
ATTACHES TO THE DRESS. WHEN
THE PARTY BEGINS, THE BRIDE
CAN REMOVE THE TRAIN FOR
BETTER MANEUVERABILITY ON
THE DANCE FLOOR.

Like other parts of the gown, the train can be enhanced with such trimmings as embroidery and beading. These adornments may run the length of the train or simply highlight the edges. For a seamless effect, the embellishments can be a continuation of a pattern that begins on the bodice. If a bride wants to dazzle her guests from behind, she may select a train covered in intricate patterns of sparkling crystals. Another bride might choose to let the rich sheen of the fabric speak for itself.

While the train is an element of the bride's gown, several members of the bridal party will determine how it looks on the big day. Page boys or trainbearers may hold the ends of the longest trains as the bride walks down the aisle (many brides prefer instead simply to let the train trail along the aisle on its own for the most breathtaking walk to the altar). The maid of honor or bridesmaids will help arrange the train into a fan shape before the bride walks down the aisle and will do the same when she arrives at the altar. The maid of honor is also a good candidate for bustling the gown after the ceremony and should accompany the bride to her final fitting in order to learn how to do so from the seamstress. Selecting the train that is right for you, and having it arranged properly, will go a long way toward ensuring that you look your best from all angles. And with a beautiful train following you down the aisle, you're bound to make a lasting impression.

RIGHT: CARE IS TAKEN TO ARRANGE A TRAIN SO THAT IT CREATES THE DESIRED EFFECT. THE FORMAL TONE SET BY THE CHAPEL TRAIN IS HEIGHTENED BY A CATHEDRAL-LENGTH TULLE VEIL, WHICH FLOATS AIRILY OVER THE DRESS AND BEYOND THE END OF THE TRAIN.

OPPOSITE: THE GROOM'S NOT PEEKING—HE'S HELPING HIS NEW BRIDE MANEUVER IN HER GOWN. A LAYER OF TULLE UNDERNEATH ADDS A BIT OF MODESTY AND STRUCTURE TO THE BALL GOWN SKIRT AND THE TRAIN.

Alfred Angelo
tel: 866-226-4356
www.alfredangelo.com

Amsale
tel: 212-971-0170
www.amsale.com

Anne Barge Collection
tel: 404-230-9995
www.annebarge.com

Carolina Herrera Ltd.
tel: 212-944-5757
www.carolinaherrerabridal.com

Christos Inc.
tel: 212-921-0025
www.christosbridal.com

Clea Colet
tel: 212-396-4608

Cynthia C. & Company
tel: 212-966-2200
www.cynthiac.com

Bridal Salon at Dayton's
tel: 612-375-2132

Galina
tel: 212-564-1020
www.galinabridal.com

Givenchy
tel: 215-659-5300
www.givenchy.com

Janell Berté Ltd.
tel: 717-291-9894

Jessica McClintock Inc.
tel: 800-711-8718
www.jessicamcclintock.com

Justina McCaffrey
tel: 888-874-GOWN
www.justinamccaffrey.com

L'Ezu Atelier
tel: 213-622-2422
www.lezu.com

Manalé
tel: 212-944-6939
www.manale.com

Melissa Sweet
tel: 859-572-9162
www.melissasweet.com

Pat Kerr
tel: 901-525-5223

Priscilla of Boston
tel: 617-242-2677
www.priscillaofboston.com

Reem Acra
tel: 212-414-0980

Tomasina
tel: 412-563-7788
www.tomasina.com

Wearkstatt
tel: 212-279-3929
www.wearkstatt.com

Alfred Angelo: pp. 2, 21, 25, 27, 30, 36, 57, 62, 72, 73, 90

Amsale: p. 20

Anne Barge Collection: ©Denis Reggie: pp. 16, 22

©**Paul Barnett:** p. 12

Carolina Herrera Ltd.: pp. 50, 53

Christos Inc.: pp. 42, 43

Clea Colet: pp. 78, 81, 85

Cynthia C. & Company: pp. 6, 11, 32, 33, 44, 49, 60, 63, 88, 89

Galina: p. 83

Givenchy: pp. 1, 29, 35, 52, 61, 77

©**Karen Hill:** pp. 74, 86

©**Lyn Hughes:** pp. 19, 70, 92

Janell Berté Ltd.: pp. 79, 84

©**Jasper-Sky:** p. 91

Jessica McClintock Inc.: p. 82

L'ezu Atelier: pp. 51, 69

Manalé: pp. 9, 23, 38, 40, 48, 56, 64, 65, 66

Justina McCaffrey, courtesy of the Bridal Salon at Dayton's: p. 18

Melissa Sweet: pp. 28, 41

©**Sarah Merians:** pp. 15, 24, 47

Pat Kerr: p. 87

Priscilla of Boston: p. 39

Reem Acra: pp. 37, 76

©**Tanya Tribble:** pp. 14, 71

Tomasina, courtesy of Modern Bride Magazine: pp. 58, 59

©**Jason Walz:** pp. 3, 45, 54, 67, 93

Wearkstatt: p. 80

ABOUT THE AUTHOR

Amy M. Nebens was a senior articles editor at *Martha Stewart Weddings* and an associate editor at *Martha Stewart Living* and *Bridal Guide* before launching her freelance career as a writer and editor. She has also written for various women's fashion and beauty magazines. Amy now lives with her husband and children in Westchester, New York.